THIS BOOK IS

Presented

TO: _____

BY: _____

ON: _____

Copyright © Arabella Penrose, 2024.

Arabella Penrose: Author, Art Director, Book Design
Frank S. Scavo: Poet, Story Editor, Collaborator
Moazam Bravi: Artwork Editor
Visionscraft: Artwork Editor

All rights reserved. No part of this publication may be reproduced, distributed, or transmitted in any form or by any means, or stored in any database or retrieval system, without prior written permission of the copyright holder.

All inquiries should be directed to:
www.arabellapenrose.com

ISBN-13: 978-1-962924-05-4 - Paperback
ISBN-13: 978-1-962924-06-1 - Hardcover

RUTH
the Moabitess

A RHYMING BIBLE STORY OF KINDNESS, LOYALTY, AND DILIGENCE

BY ARABELLA PENROSE

"Ruth said,
'Don't urge me to leave you,
and to return from following you,
for where you go, I will go;
and where you stay, I will stay.
Your people will be my people,
and your God my God.'"

Ruth 1:16 (WEB)

For all the women waiting for their "Boaz."
May you find him in Christ.

¶In the country of Moab, so far from God's land,
Lived Ruth, who knew not of God's people or plan.

She married a young man,
a Jew named Mahlon,

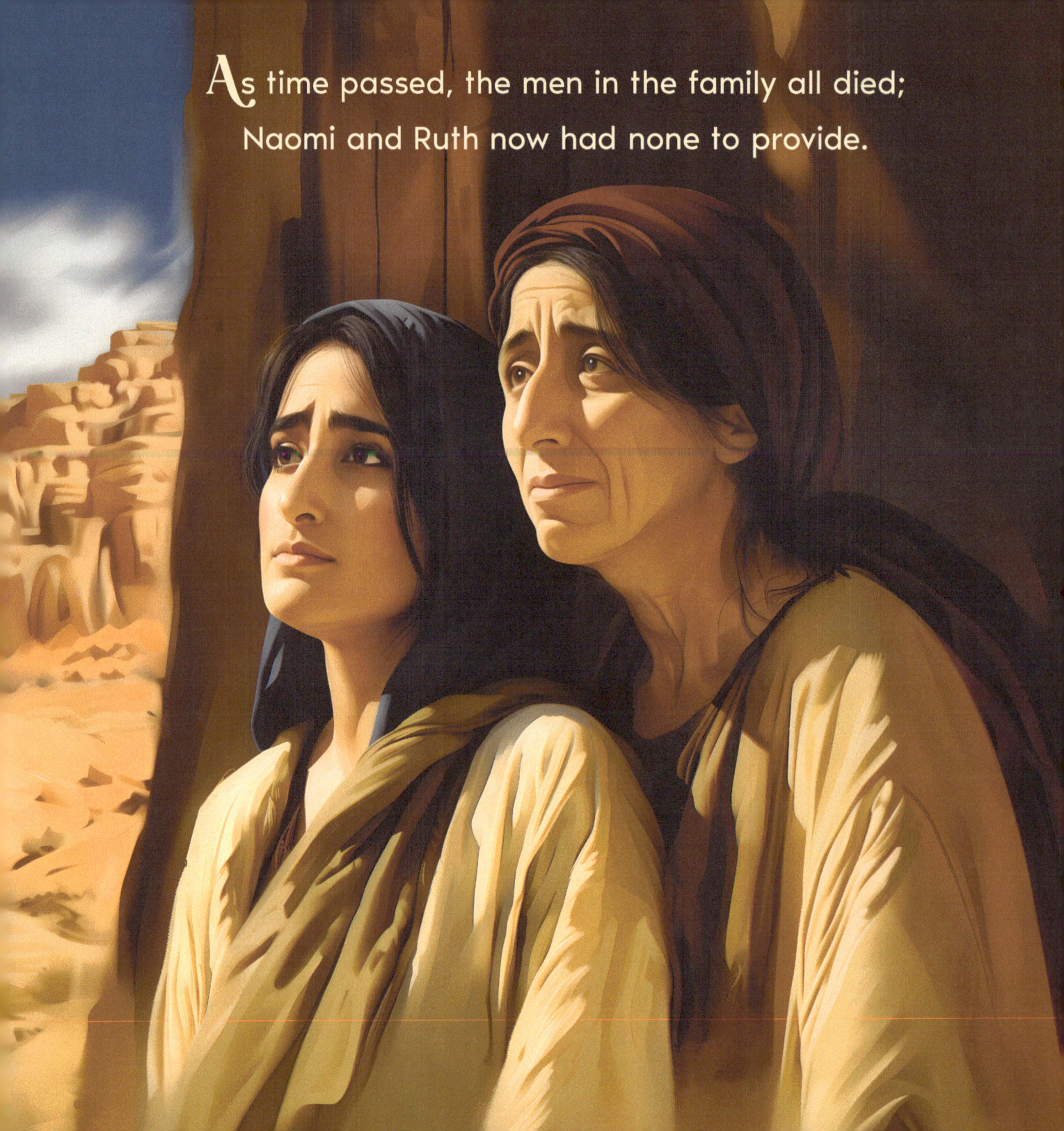

As time passed, the men in the family all died;
Naomi and Ruth now had none to provide.

But Ruth to Naomi cried, "Don't make me leave,"
I'll go where you go, and to you I will cleave.
And where you will stay, I'll stay always with you;
Your people be mine, and your God, my God, too."

Read: Ruth 1:16-18

And so, they arose and to Bethlehem went,
Exhausted and hungry, their money all spent.

But the harvest of barley had started, they'd seen,
So Ruth went to find her some grain she could glean.

Read: Ruth 1:22, 2:1-2

A relative, Boaz, a field he did own.
He felt Ruth deserved to have mercy be shown.

"I heard what you did for Naomi, my kin;
The Lord now reward you, take you under His wing."

Read: Ruth 2:3, 11-12

So, Ruth and Naomi were now fully fed.
Naomi rejoiced in God's blessing and said,
"May God now bless Boaz, his grace he has shown;
And as a redeemer to us be he known."

For their husbands had died, and no heirs were alive;
The family name had no way to survive.
So they needed a kinsman to come alongside,
And purchase the land of their husbands who'd died.

Read: Ruth 2:20, Leviticus 25:25

Naomi told Ruth, "Dress your finest tonight.
Find Boaz, seek favor from him in his sight.
For he is a relative, ever esteemed;
Ask him to protect us, that we be redeemed."

Read: Ruth 3:1-6

Read: Ruth 3:7-9

"God bless you, my daughter, your kindness is vast.
Do not be afraid, I'll do all that you ask.
Yet there is a relative, closer than me,
But if he's not willing, your redeemer I'll be."

Read: Ruth 3:10-13

The next day, then, Boaz went to the town gate.
He spoke to that kinsman concerning Ruth's fate.
"Redeem the estate, and it all will be yours.
But you must marry Ruth, so the family endures."

He said, "Yes, I would like that land to be mine.
But I won't marry Ruth, though I am first in line.
I think it be best that you now marry her,
To be their redeemer, their name to secure."

Read: Ruth 4:1-8

So, Boaz took Ruth, and his wife she became,
With hope that the family's name would remain.

Ruth gave birth to Obed, a new baby boy;
And he was to Naomi a son and a joy.

Read: Ruth 4:13-16

And as the years passed,
the family name became great,
As Obed's son, Jesse,
received the estate.

And Jesse's son David
to the throne he ascended,

And from David, Christ Jesus, our Redeemer, descended.

A woman so noble, like Ruth, who can find:
So hard-working, loyal, so thoughtful, and kind?
And when Boaz found her, he showed her such care;
Together they brought forth the family heir.

Read: Proverbs 31:10

So let us, like Ruth, work with kindness and grace.
Have courage with love, and God's people embrace.
Believe in Christ Jesus, and never forget:
Like Boaz, He saved us, and paid all our debt.

Discussion Guide

LOYALTY AND LOVE

Question: Why did Ruth decide to stay with Naomi instead of going back to her own family?

Discuss: Explain loyalty as sticking by someone even when it's difficult. Discuss how Ruth's decision shows her strong commitment and love for Naomi. Ask your child if they can think of a time when they showed loyalty to someone they care about.

KINDNESS OF RUTH

Question: How was Ruth a kind person?

Discuss: Ruth showed kindness to Naomi. After their husbands both died, Naomi told Ruth to go back to her family. But Ruth chose to stay with Naomi and take care of her. Can your child give any examples of kindness they have seen in their own life?

KINDNESS OF BOAZ

Question: How did Boaz show kindness to Ruth?

Discuss: Highlight Boaz's generosity in allowing Ruth to glean in his fields and protecting her. Discuss how we can be kind to newcomers or those in need.

HARDWORK AND DILIGENCE

Question: How did Ruth show diligence in the story?

Discuss: Explain diligence as working hard and not giving up. Point out how Ruth worked in the fields to provide for herself and Naomi. Discuss why it's important to work hard and how your child can show diligence at home or in school.

FAITHFULNESS

Question: How did Ruth show faithfulness to Naomi?

Discuss: Highlight Ruth's words: "Your people will be my people, and your God my God." Discuss the idea of faithfulness to family and faith. Talk about age-appropriate ways to express faith, such as prayer, kindness to others, or participating in worship.

BRAVERY AND COURAGE

Question: How was Ruth brave in the story?

Discuss: Discuss Ruth's courage in leaving her home and following Naomi's instructions on how to approach Boaz. Talk about what bravery means and share examples of when your child has shown courage, even in small ways.

HELPING OTHERS

Question: Why is it important to be helpful in your family?

Discuss: Discuss how families work together and support each other. Explore ways your child can contribute to family life. Talk about how Boaz helped Ruth and Naomi, and how helping others can lead to good things.

GOD'S PLAN

Question: How did Ruth and Boaz's kindness to each other lead to something good?

Discuss: Explain how their kindness led to their marriage and the continuation of the family line, eventually leading to King David and Jesus. Discuss the idea that everyone has a special purpose in God's plan and ask your child what they think their special purpose might be.

ROLE MODELS

Question: If you could be like Ruth in one way, what would it be?

Discuss: Discuss traits like loyalty, kindness, hard work, and faithfulness. Encourage your child to choose a positive trait from Ruth's character and talk about how they might apply this trait in their own life.

TO GET **FREE PRINTABLE DOWNLOADS**
OF THE DISCUSSION GUIDE AND OTHER FREE RESOURCES,
GO TO MY **WEBSITE:** **WWW.ARABELLAPENROSE.COM**

About the Series

In a world filled with conflicting messages about femininity, the "Real Women Heroes of the Bible" series brings biblical role models to life for today's generation. Told in rhyming verse, each book tells of a different biblical heroine, showcasing their unique virtues and traits. The series features realistic illustrations that convey these are real women, not fairy tales. By exploring the lives of these women God intentionally chose to be featured in His Word, young girls can find godly examples of womanhood and be inspired to develop their own God-given strengths. Most importantly, they will understand that the very best models for what it means to be a woman can be found in the pages of the Bible. Each heroine's faith-filled life carries powerful lessons that will speak to the hearts of girls today.

About the Author

Since childhood, Arabella has always loved poetry and dreamed of one day publishing her own poems. She splits her time between her native Southern California and Southern Spain. After earning her Bachelor of Arts from UC Santa Barbara, Arabella worked as a translator and a teacher. But her true passion is to nurture the hearts of children through stories. In her spare time, you can find Arabella hiking or walking the beach with her pup, Snoopy, and spending time with her son, Mateo. Arabella draws inspiration from her father, who instilled in her a love of poetry and scripture. She hopes to glorify God with her stories and inspire the next generation to discover the transformative power of God's Word.

COLLECT THE WHOLE SERIES!

To get updates on new releases,
sign up for my newsletter at www.arabellapenrose.com

Thank You!

Dear reader,

I hope reading this rhyming bible story inspired you and your child as much as it did me in writing it.

If you found value in this book, please consider leaving an honest review on Amazon or Goodreads. Your feedback helps other families discover meaningful books. And, by sharing your thoughts, you encourage me to continue writing stories that nurture little hearts.

Thank you for reading this timeless tale of Ruth with your child. I'm grateful for readers like you.

Blessings,

Arabella Penrose

HAVE A PRAYER REQUEST
or want to reach out?
Email me at arabella@arabellapenrose.com

www.ingramcontent.com/pod-product-compliance
Lightning Source LLC
Chambersburg PA
CBHW041405010526
44107CB00015B/1084